12 Step Approach to Sponsorships

The Step-By-Step Guide To Acquiring Sponsors & Maintaining Relationships

By Lynn F. Austin

Copyright © 2016 Austin Group Consulting
All rights reserved.

ISBN:
978-0-9973227-4-3
978-0-9973227-5-0
978-0-9973227-6-7

This book is dedicated to my family, friends and clients.

12 Step Approach to Sponsorships

Table of Contents

1. Brand Image
2. Research
3. Budget
4. Metrics
5. Proposal
6. Distribution
7. Negotiate Terms
8. Agreements
9. Relationships
10. Marketing
11. Commitments
12. Results / Reporting

Acknowledgements

Thank you to my supporters, mentors and coaches. This book would not have been possible without the tireless encouragement of my community of accountabilities partners from the Ultimate Success Masterclass.

I would also like to thank Nedra Keener for editing assistance, and Lorenzo Benton and Carla Adams for support and input during the early conference workshops.

About The Author

Lynn F. Austin, MBA is an adjunct professor at Grand Canyon University, managing director at Austin Group Consulting, LLC – A marketing, public relations, media and executive leader-ship consulting firm founded to coach, guide and empower personal and business brand strategy evolution; effective communication mastery; executive press/media interview skill enhancement, and transformational leadership development. Ms. Austin's professional portfolio includes

executive and leadership roles at Aston Martin, Jaguar, Land Rover and Harley-Davidson Mo-tor Company. Among her many professional accolades, Lynn was the first African American Director of Marketing at Harley-Davidson Motor Company.

After more than 20 years working for Fortune 500 companies with responsibilities reviewing and approving sponsorships for small, large and non profit organizations, she developed this workshop series to help others crack the code in getting their programs funded.

Lynn has taught this workshop throughout the country for organizations like National Coalition of 100 Black Women, Bikers Empowerment Training Conference and others.

She enjoys riding motorcycles, hiking, reading, traveling and spending time with family and friends.

Introduction

Thank you for purchasing this ebook designed to help you learn how to get sponsorship funding for your programs, events and activities. I realize there are many other resources out there competing for your attention, and appreci-ate you entrusting me to help you reach your goals.

After spending nearly 20 years in leadership roles at Fortune 100 companies with responsibilities for implementing multi-million dollar marketing cam-paigns where I rejected and approved sponsorship proposals for every imag-inable type of program from kids school events to multi-city music tours and beyond, I decided to develop a workshop to "crack the code" on what actually works when it comes to getting programs sponsored.

The inspiration behind writing this ebook was to educate people as well as save them valuable time, energy and frustration in getting companies and or-ganizations to sponsor their programs, events and activities. In this ebook, I share with you inside information to "crack the code" so that you can achieve the same results as many who have learned and applied these tips from my workshops.

In this ebook, you'll learn a 12 Step process for winning sponsorships in-cluding how to 1) identify the best companies to target for your program; 2) develop and deliver a compelling proposal; 3) to negotiate to get to the "yes"; 4) capture and present the right measurements; and 5) maintain good and effective relationships for future sponsorship opportunities.

12 Step Approach to Sponsorships

What You Can Expect to Learn

- "Crack the Code" on how to get sponsorship funding for your programs
- Learn what sponsors require to approve proposal requests
- Learn the importance of your brand image
- Understand the "value" in your brand and how to leverage it
- Learn how to research companies to create a prospect list of sponsors
- Learn the timing and methods for contacting sponsors
- Learn the value of tracking, measuring and reporting your results
- Learn about sponsorship package pricing, entitlements and customization
- Learn techniques for negotiating and getting to win/win terms and agreements
- Learn what you need to know about when, where and how to distribute your proposal

Questions to Consider as You Begin

While you likely do not have the answers to these questions when you start, it is beneficial to consider them as you begin planning to help guide you as you proceed through each step.

1. What type of activity are you doing?
2. Why (purpose) are you doing it?
3. How/what kind of activity will you do?
4. Who benefits and how?
5. Where will it be? (location, venue)
6. How long is it? (hours, days)
7. How much will it cost?
8. How much do I want to make/profit?
9. What marketing approach will you use?

With that, let's get started "cracking the code."

Step One

Brand Image

12 Step Approach to Sponsorships

Step One: Brand Image

Brand: Your brand represents who and what you stand for in the marketplace.

Brand Image: Your brand image is the impression current or potential "customers" have about your product. Note: This can include "real" or "imaginary" qualities or shortcomings.

Brand Management: Brand management involves everything from your brand name, its attributes, where/how its positioned (yours vs someone else) as well as sustaining and maintaining what the brand promises and then maintaining that promise.

Things to Note

- What is your brand's image?
    - What do you represent, what are your values
- Protect, build and value your brand so that it is true to and maintains what it promises
- Value how your brand is presented everyday and in everyway, to ev-eryone…treat your brand with respect so that others will understand and believe in to too.
- Prospective sponsor will look to your brand's equity (overall value) in considering aligning, partnering or sponsoring your program, service or activity.

Step Two

Research

12 Step Approach to Sponsorships

Step Two: Research

It is important to research and understand the companies you will approach for sponsorship consideration. The more you know about the company, and their view on sponsoring programs, the better your chances are to secure support.

- Use the Internet or other resources to research potential companies and partnerships that match your group or organizations brand image, values, and interests.

- Consider businesses you use often, i.e., Service shops, dealerships, gas companies, insurance companies, hotels

- Research companies with products targeting specific groups like, women, men, athletic, youth, children, adult, etc.

- Inquire about each company's process and timing for accepting, re-viewing, and awarding proposals, i.e., are budgets set annually, quarterly, monthly; does the company review proposals annually or during fiscal budgeting cycle

- Start and maintain a database of all companies researched. Include notes indicating why they are a good prospect and/or why they are not a good prospect at the time. This helps to qualify the prospects you will approach.

Step Three

Budget

12 Step Approach to Sponsorships

Step Three: Budget

It is essential to establish, so that you have a clear understanding of your overall costs, expenses, desired revenue, and so that you establish sufficient funding amounts to cover all in pricing your sponsorship levels.

What is your budget?

- List all of your known and anticipated costs/expenses
  - The venue, entertainment, activities, permits, insurance, promo-tional items/giveaways, porta johns, security, staff, support, charita-ble giving – list everything you can think of – even if you don't know the actual cost at this point.

- How much money do you need?
  - To breakeven, to donate, to pay staff, to make a profit?

Note: Depending on the type of event, reach, and size -- consider media partners as a way to reduce promotional budget and/or to decrease expenses paid. (include your overall budget and/or decrease expenses paid.)

Step Four

★ ★ ★

Metrics

★ ★ ★

12 Step Approach to Sponsorships

Step Four: Metrics

How you intend to measure the success of your event can be an important factor in approving your proposal. Look for ways that meet your idea of an good event as well as the company's measurement of success for an event, i.e.,

- Consider what you might need to *measure* or track both for you and the prospective sponsor (builds value and interest):

    - Return on Investment (ROI): If company wants customer lead-cards (customer information) they may estimate the success of your event by calculating the cost of their sponsorship fee by number of leads your event can get (give to them).

        - $5,000 sponsorship/1000 leads = $5.00/lead

- Return on Objective (ROO): Can you achieve (do) what you say you can do, i.e. # of attendees, # of leads, # of sampling, amount of media exposure, etc. *Consider the "Quality" of Leads*

- *Are there other important metrics to be considered – branding, awareness, exposure, etc.*

    - How/when will you be expected to share results?

- *During the event, 30, 60, 90 days after the event?*

Step Five

Proposal

12 Step Approach to Sponsorships

Step Five: Proposal

Begin proposal by outlining information about your brand, what you stand for, why you're doing program, how long the it has existed:

- Be clear and truthful about what you are doing and what you can deliver.
- At a minimum, your proposal should include:
    - An overview or summary of your program (this statement may be the first impression of you and your program, be clear and concise).
    - Your objectives for the program (why you are doing it, what you expect to accomplish, i.e., charity, donation, scholarship, etc.
    - What you need from a sponsor (how much will it cost them)

    - How you are going to execute the event (methodology)
    - What you are going to do (top line execution plan)
    - A profile of expected attendees (target audience or demographics (race, sex, age, average income, etc. Companies generally want to know where their funds will be going and if your program helps them reach their desired targets.
- Think Win/Win:
    - What does a successful program look like for you AND your pro-spective sponsor.
        - Educate companies on why they should "want/need" to sponsor your program: *If they are looking at other programs, give them a reason to consider yours over another.*
- *Develop sponsorship levels/packages that make sense for your type of program that will interest prospective sponsors, i.e., title, presenting, entertainment, etc.*

Step Six

Distribution

12 Step Approach to Sponsorships

Step Six: Distribution

Present your proposal to the prospective sponsor/ company representative you researched previously, Remember:

- Know the process for accepting/reviewing/awarding proposals for the "qualified" companies identified.

- Follow their directions for submitting proposals. i.e., Internet, paper, etc.

    - Call in advance if you are unaware.

    - Request a meeting if possible to try to present your proposal in person or by conference call.

    - Mail, email, deliver a meeting, is not an available option.

        - If you mail, follow up by phone or email and ask for a time to review or get feedback on your proposal

- Keep a log and follow-up with a phone call on all submitted proposals.

    - Note any "no's" you get

        - Pay attention to your "no's" and change your proposal if nec-essary so that you can increase the chances of getting a yes, when you ask them in the future.

        - Remember: No may not always mean (no-never), it may just mean no, not right now; not this budget cycle; not this year. It is important to understand so that you have a better chance for yes in the future.

Submitting Proposals - Timing/Method

- Organizations receive many requests for support or sponsorship. Submit your proposal early to get the best chances for getting a "YES."

- Remember to consider the company's budgeting cycle:

    - Calendar year budgeting cycle: The organization may only review/consider proposal requests August – November for funding during the next calendar year.

    - Fiscal year budgeting cycle: The organization may only consider proposal requests March – May for the upcoming fiscal year.

    - Quarterly budgeting cycle: The organization may consider request more frequently, reviewing request the prior quarter – for funding during an upcoming quarter.

- Some organization may accept paper or email proposals, while an increasing number will only accept proposals through an online submis-sion system often accessible from their website. If you don't know how the organization you are interested receives/approves sponsorships it is best to call to ask or confirm that their process has not changed .

Step Seven

Negotiate Terms

Step Seven: Negotiate Terms

Sponsorship package levels may be generic or "cookie-cuter" to start, but most prospective sponsors like to be able to customize their options:

- Be Flexible

- Be Creative and Offer Suggested Options for Consideration

- Consider expense items you may be able to barter or trade for services. It is important to know what you need and what you may be able to give to receive it. (refer to expense items in budget)

    - Printing, media, etc.

- Negotiate Acceptable Terms:

    - Allow prospective sponsor ways to customize their investment in your program.

    - Discuss terms "negotiate" early to optimize opportunities for win/win

    - Suggest opportunities for prospective sponsor to share levels if applicable.

Step Eight

Agreements

Step Eight: Agreements

Remember to think Win/Win…think about success – for your program and for the prospective sponsor.

Ask for and/or get agreement from the prospective sponsor on "what a successful program" looks like.

- Agree on how you will provide data/results from the program in advance.

- Agree on what the company measures: ROI, ROO, leads, awareness, etc.

- Agree on the company's desired outcome (objective) for the program?

Do not include anything in the agreement that you cannot or don't believe you can deliver just to secure the sponsorship.

- Remember you always want to build long-term value in your program as your organization or program's reputation is at stake!

Step Nine

Relationships

Step Nine: Relationships

CONGRATULATIONS!!! The prospective sponsor has agreed to sponsor your program. Now what?

- Value relationships with your sponsors.

    - Commit to and keep the agreed project timelines for your program.

    - Be timely and responsive to your sponsors inquiries before, during and after your program.

        - Keep your sponsor in the loop of important developments, particularly if it affects the outcome of the event or their level of participation. They should never be the LAST TO KNOW.

    - Manage your budget – costs and expenses

        - This will help ensure you reach your desired financial goals and allow you to show financial responsibility to your sponsors.

Step Ten

Marketing

Step Ten: Marketing

How will you market your program

- Television or Radio
- Website Presence
- Social Media Presence
- Street Teams
- Videos
- Other grass roots advertising, media and/or promotional activities
- Etc.

Television/Radio – Have an idea of listeners, frequency etc. for where you will be placing advertising as well as the amount of exposure the sponsor will get with these advertising buys. Of course the more sponsorship revenue - more potential media buys and better ad placement. So it is important to understand the value.

Website Presence – If you are able to and have committed, include sponsor's logo or other company information as agreed, as well as your information on their website if possible.

Social Media Presence – Social media value can be in the number of followers, fans, website registered users or the number of people you can quantify that you can "tell" about the program. I.e., Facebook, Twitter, Yelp, Myspace, Instagram, YouTube, Google+, etc.

Videos – Videos can be powerful to tell what is going on, when, who is involved and why. Consider making videos and posting to social media or sending via email campaigns to further market your program.

Step Eleven

Commitments

Step Eleven: Commitments

- Follow-through on promises and commitments made to your sponsors

- Get feedback from sponsors (in writing if possible) on success of your program

  - Plan a debrief meeting to get feedback. This is valuable for future events & securing new sponsors

- Ask early for renewals/recommitment

- Include positive feedback received in next proposal where appropriate

  - Try to get a good quote, testimonial or letter of support from your sponsors about your program that you can add to future proposals

Step Twelve

Results

Step Twelve: Results / Reporting

Following your program, deliver your wrap up report on what went well, opportunities for improvement (if applicable), number of attendees, list, etc.:

- Deliver a wrap up report or final count data to your sponsor in a timely manner following the program
- Provide details and information on mailing lists, number of leads, impressions, attendees, etc. outlined in your agreement.
- *Request a copy of their final assessment of your program*
    - Be aware of what sponsors think of your program.
    - Know the value your sponsor places on helping them to achieve their objectives
- Get your sponsor's opinion or assessment of your program.
- NOTE: This insight can be quite valuable in promoting your program to request future support and to acquire new sponsors.

12 Step Approach to Sponsorships

Wrap Up

Among the many benefits of successfully acquiring sponsorships for your programs, events or activities, they can also help to: enhance your brand; raise awareness of the types of programs and activities you're involved with; provide companies with opportunities to get to niche or specialty markets that you may have access to; generate revenue for your programs, etc.

Be diligent with your brand and its image. Companies you approach for sponsorship are more likely to consider aligning with your brand, if your brand's values align, compliment or support their organizational mission and vision. Ensure that your brand image is what you want it to be and an image potential sponsors would want to align with.

As indicated, companies receive many proposals and request for sponsorship of various types of activities. Taking the time to: 1) do your research so that you prepare a proposal with a clear understanding of your budget, success measures and how you will market; 2) confidently negotiate terms to get to agreement; 3) honor commitments; and 4) communicate results will help your request stand out among most in its thoroughness and attention to detail that the sponsor doesn't have to try to figure out. Thank you again for purchasing this ebook. Following the 12-steps listed here will equip you with the necessary tools to acquire sponsorships and maintain good relationships with your sponsors.

"One important key to success is self-confidence. An important key to self-confidence is preparation."

— Arthur Ashe

Resources

Marketing/Promotion Toolbox Items

Brand Management: Be mindful and protective of brand. You want companies to desire partnering with you and your brand and can see the benefits for their brand

Advertising: Generally paid form of communication with non- personal ideas, goods or services designed to increase brand awareness, opinion or consideration. Some channels include (but not limited to):

- TV/Cable
- Print
- Internet/social media
- Billboards

Personal Sales/Ticket Sales: Personal pitch to make sales and build relationships

- Word of mouth
- Street Teams
- Tickets Sold

Direct Marketing: Making direct connections with targeted groups or individuals

- Flyers
- Booths at trade show, conferences, conventions
- Telemarketing (making calls)
- Email (individual or campaigns)

Cold Contact Cover Letter Template

[Date]

[Name]
[Title]
[Company]
[Address]
[City, State Zip Code]

Dear [NAME]:

I am writing to offer [PROSPECT COMPANY] sponsorship opportunities with [YOUR PROGRAM] [YOUR CITY].

[YOUR PROGRAM] is [BRIEF DESCRIPTION OF ORGANIZATION]. [YOUR PROGRAM] brings together [#] of [TYPE OR TARGET AUDIENCE] for [BRIEF COMMENT ON WHAT TO EXPECT AT EVENT]. Sponsorship of the event offers opportunities to promote your brand, access a coveted demographic, offer product samplings, build on your positive community image, and provide unique customized opportunities.

[YOUR PROGRAM] will be held on [date of event], at [name of venue] in [YOUR city]. Since [INAUGURAL YEAR], our event has raised [$XXX,XXX] to support [CAUSE – IF APPLICABLE]. With the support of our sponsors, we are able to [ADD BENEFITS IF PROCEEDS ARE SUPPORTING A CAUSE].   [NOTE IF NO PREVIOUS INFO, INDICATE WHAT YOU HOPE TO DO]

I have attached a one-page summary of our event. We hope that you will join us in [INSERT CAUSE], and take advantage of the excellent opportunities offered through [YOUR PROGRAM\. I will follow up with you on [DATE]. If you have any questions before then, please don't hesitate to contact me.

Sincerely,

[Your Name]
[Title on Committee]
[Your detailed contact information]

Proposal Worksheet

EXEUCTIVE SUMMARY
Who are you/what is your organization:
What do you do/type of organization:
What type of event or activity are you doing:
Why are you doing it?

WHY SHOULD A COMPANY SPONSOR YOUR PROGRAM
What's in it for the sponsor:
How does your program help sponsor achieve objectives: What's in it for you:
Are you a non-profit or is a non profit benefiting:

WHAT IS THE AUDIENCE BREAKDOWN/DEMOGRAPHICS

Women: Men: Children:
Ethnicity: Education:
Employment: Income:
Other:

WHAT ARE YOU PLANNING FOR THE PROGRAM

Sampling: Workshops: Seminars:
Awards: Contests: Fashion
Show:
Other:

HOW MUCH WILL IT COST THE COMPANY
Design sponsor packages, i.e., platinum, gold, silver, bronze

WHAT DOES THE COMPANY GET
List entitlements, i.e., access to mailing lists, tickets, signage, advertising, etc.

HOW WILL YOU MARKET
List how you will spread the work about your program, social media, website, tv, radio

HOW WILL SUCCESS BE MEASURES
List what a successful program would look like, $$ raised for charity, attendance, leads, etc.

WHO IS THE CONTACT PERSON
List who the company should contact regarding the proposal

12 STEP Quick Reference Card

A 12-Step Approach to Sponsorship

Step 1: Brand Image - Credibility/Value/Equity

Step 2: Research Partnerships

Step 3: Establish Budget

Step 4: Define Measurement/Metrics

Step 5: Draft Proposal

Step 6: Distribute/Present Your Proposal

Step 7: Negotiating Terms

Step 8: Reach Agreements

Step 9: Manage Relationship

Step 10: Marketing Your Event

Step 11: Keep Commitments

Step 12: Reporting Results

Sponsorships?

Contact us for a Free 30 Minute Consultation

info@austingroupconsulting.com

www.austingroupconsulting.com

www.ingramcontent.com/pod-product-compliance
Lightning Source LLC
Chambersburg PA
CBHW041756040426
42446CB00001B/50